My Life In Colors

Embracing the Rainbow

BY ROBERTO JIMENEZ

My Life In Colors
Embracing the Rainbow

ROBERTO JIMENEZ

StoryTerrace

Design Mitar Stjepcevic, on behalf of StoryTerrace

Copyright © Roberto Jimenez

First print September 2022

StoryTerrace

www.StoryTerrace.com

CONTENTS

PART 1: EGG — 7
1. WHO I AM — 15
2. LIFE IN THE DOMINICAN REPUBLIC — 19

PART 2: CATERPILLAR — 27
3. COMING TO THE USA — 29
4. LIFE IN NEW YORK — 33

PART 3: CHRYSALIS — 41
5. COLLEGE YEARS — 47
6. COMING OUT — 59
7. FINDING MYSELF — 69
8. CHALLENGES ALONG THE WAY — 75

PART 4: BUTTERFLY — 87
9. MY LIFE — 95
10. MY WORK — 109
11. WORDS OF WISDOM — 117

PART 1

EGG

MY LIFE IN COLORS

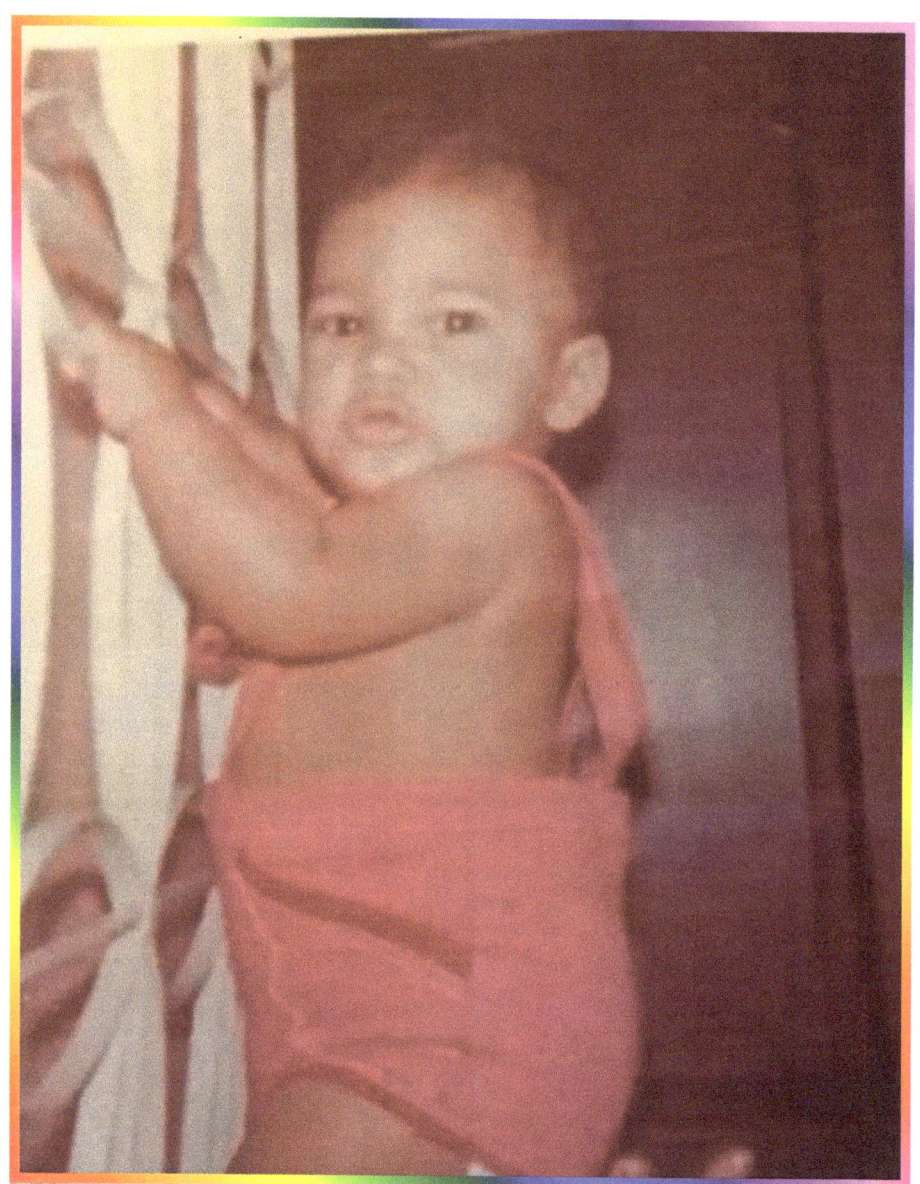

Me as an infant in DR.

MY LIFE IN COLORS

Bio parents
Childhood

MY LIFE IN COLORS

1-year-old Me

MY LIFE IN COLORS

My oldest brother (Richard) and I. My paternal grandmother (Dona Emma) was carrying me,

MY LIFE IN COLORS

1
WHO I AM

This is a story about me: Dr. Roberto Rafael Jimenez. If you're reading this, you might know me already. If you do, I hope this lets you know me better. If you don't know me yet, I hope you get to know me a little bit here. I've been through a lot in my 48 years on this earth. I am an immigrant and the first man in my family to come out as gay. I've worked hard my whole life and put myself through college to get multiple degrees, including my doctorate. It's been a long but rewarding journey.

The first thing you need to know about me is that I am not shy. In fact, I have no filter whatsoever. I'm not argumentative, but I'm not afraid to ask questions or to say whatever I'm thinking. This has served me well in life but has also occasionally gotten me into some trouble. For instance, growing up Catholic in the Dominican Republic, I went to catechism classes to prepare for my first communion. Even as a kid, I had a lot of questions. Why do we do things this way and not another? What does baptizing babies do when they have no say in the matter? Stuff like that. So, I asked these questions straight to the priest. Needless to say, the priest didn't find my questions charming. He accused me of being disrespectful and threw me out of class. Multiple times.

Each time, he sent me home to my mother, informing her that I would not be receiving my first communion until I could learn to accept the lessons without endless questioning. My mom was even less amused than the priest. Angrily, she told me to stop living in my head and to just accept what I was told and say what they wanted me to say. But that's just not my way! So I never did finish my catechism classes as a kid. I didn't do my first communion until I was an adult at St. Thomas University.

But I am who I am. I'm a curious, emotional, and expressive person. That same curious nature that got me into some hot water from time to time has also brought me to where I am today: Thriving in Miami, Florida. I have been in a loving relationship with the same man for 28 years, whom I am proud to call my husband. I am a licensed marriage and family therapist, have a doctorate in education, leadership, and management, and run my own private practice. I have found a way to live life on my terms and my terms alone.

However, the road to getting here has not always been an easy one. Growing up, I had no real role models—at least none who were outwardly living the life I wanted for myself. I often felt strange and alone in the ways I thought and the ways I felt. I spent a lot of my young life hiding from myself and from others. It took me a long time to find the courage to move past that and carve my own way.

So, if you want to get to know me better or if you see some of yourself reflected in what is written above, read on. Either way, I am excited to share my journey with you. I hope you find something in these pages to inspire you.

My Dad!

2

LIFE IN THE DOMINICAN REPUBLIC

I was born in Santo Domingo in the Dominican Republic on January 30th, 1974. I was the middle child of three boys born to my father, Roberto Jimenez, and my mother, Andreina Madera. My older brother, Richard, was only 11 months older than me, and my younger brother, Ricky, was 12 years younger. Later, I would come to have more siblings from my father's side (there are 12 of us in total) whom I love very much, but these were the brothers I lived with in the DR.

We had a nice life in the DR. My father had a good job and was respected in the community. My mother was the favorite daughter of a successful businessman. We always had enough money and lived comfortably. We were sent to private school and had the resources to join extracurricular clubs and take extra classes.

My mother and father were both very loving but polar opposites. My mother was strict and no-nonsense. She was very direct and always spoke her mind. My father was more gentle and emotional. He always took a softer tone. He was inclined to comfort, while my mother was more inclined to discipline. Despite their different approaches to parenting, I never had any doubt that both of them loved me and my brothers very much.

My memories from that time are mostly happy ones. I spent most of my time with my brother, Richard. Even though we were very different, he was my best friend. He was tall, athletic, and rebellious, while I was chubby, cute, and emotional. He always looked out for me and wouldn't let anybody mess with me.

One day, when I was about five or six, my parents went out on a date and left Richard and me in the care of an aunt. She was interested in a boy who was having a birthday party that day, so she dragged us along with her. We didn't know anybody there. We were bored and felt out of place. Richard decided he had had enough, so he took me by the hand and led me out into the streets of Santo Domingo to find an adventure of our own.

Of course, we got lost. We wandered around the city by ourselves until dark. At one point, a strange man tried to grab us out on the street, but we managed to run away from him. Even though it should have been a scary experience for someone so young, I remember feeling like everything would be OK because I had Richard with me. I knew he would always take care of me. Eventually, hours later, Richard recognized the gate on one of the houses we passed as that of the house of our godfather. We went up to the house, and our godfather let us in. The police had been looking for us, and our parents were absolutely terrified. He called them, and they came to get us.

From that day on, they were extremely protective, and my brother and I lived a fairly sheltered life. We were never allowed to make close friends and were always expected to stay with the family. We were even assigned a driver, who was really more like a cross between a babysitter and bodyguard. He went with us everywhere and watched over us every second. Because of that, it was hard to get into too much trouble. The driver was always there to step in if we started to get out of line.

Outside of family time, school was the only other place I really went. My brother and I both went to Colegio Loyola, a private Catholic school in Santo Domingo. The education the school provided was very good, but the school did not allow for any diversity or difference among its students. You were expected to conform. You wore the uniform and behaved the way they wanted you to. This was a problem for me. I didn't behave the way boys my age were expected to behave. I talked differently. I stood differently. I wanted to play with different toys and play different games from the other boys. Because of this, I was often punished at school for acting "too feminine."

I became very attached to one of my male classmates. We spent a lot of time together. We were always playing together and ate our lunches together. We were inseparable. My teachers and my family were concerned about our relationship. They thought we were growing closer than they felt two young boys should be, so they tried to separate us as often as they could. On the day of a school picnic, I was very excited for my family to meet him. He was my best friend at school, and I was sure that once they met him, everything would be fine. But after seeing us together, my father pulled me aside and told me, very softly, that I couldn't be friends with him anymore. He didn't like how closely we played together.

The next day at school, when my friend invited me to lunch, I told him we couldn't be friends anymore. I was used to doing what my parents asked of me, so I never questioned it. I didn't even wait around to see his reaction. I just left and didn't talk to him again. Later, I saw him eating lunch by himself, and it made me sad. I missed him. I could see that he was sad too, and I felt bad that I had hurt him. But I loved and respected my dad, and I wanted to obey his wishes. So I stayed away.

Things that the adults in my life were concerned about didn't change, though. My family felt that I was still acting too feminine. They were beginning to worry that I was a homosexual and blamed it on the notion that I wasn't getting enough discipline at the Catholic school. So I was sent to military school, where they thought they could discipline my "feminine qualities" out of me.

MY LIFE IN COLORS

My experience at Academia Militar Del Caribe was very different from Loyola. It was extremely structured and much less religious. I was still often bullied for being too feminine (they called me "mujer" as a way to insult me), but I learned to adapt and make friends. I liked the uniforms we wore and thought they were very stylish. They used exercise as a form of punishment, so I started to lose a little weight. I even grew accustomed to the yelling. It toughened me up a little bit and gave me something to prove. I worked hard in my classes and made it onto the honor roll.

But all this time, I stayed who I was. I started to realize that I liked boys around eighth grade, but because I knew it wouldn't be accepted, I kept it to myself. I was still expressive and creative and tried my best to find outlets for that. But my parents and teachers thought that creative pursuits were a waste of time. I remember one summer my mom asked Richard and me what we wanted to do for our summer activities. Richard wanted to play basketball, which was of course no problem. I wanted to do theater.

"No, pick something else," my mother said.

"Art!" was my next suggestion.

"No, something else."

This went back and forth for a while until we eventually decided that I would take up swimming, and I enrolled with my cousin Yvonne. It turned out to suit me just fine. I was good at swimming, even though no one expected me to be. Plus, all the boys wore speedos, so I was *very* comfortable with the whole thing. We used to stop after classes to get sweets at the Sweet Candy Shop.

Life went on this way for the first 13 years of my life. It wasn't perfect, but I found a way to live as authentically as I could. In general, I was doing well. Little did I know that everything was about to be turned completely upside-down.

MY LIFE IN COLORS

Childhood in DR
Paternal Granddad - Roberto Jimenez Sr.
Me - Academia Del Caribe

PART 2

CATERPILLAR

3

COMING TO THE USA

One night, when I was 13 years old, my parents gathered all of us together for a family meeting. They informed me and my brothers that they were planning on getting a divorce. My father was going to stay in the Dominican Republic, while my mother was planning on moving to the United States to be closer to her family. She would be taking my younger brother, Ricky, with her. My older brother, Richard, immediately decided to stay with our dad in the DR.

When it was my turn to announce my decision, I was speechless (which, for me, is a very unusual thing). I now had an impossible choice to make. Richard was my best friend and my closest companion. I loved my father dearly, but I felt closer to my mother. I was completely torn. I liked my life in the DR, but something bad had happened to me there. When I was around five years old, I was sexually molested by someone I trusted. The experience was traumatic and had stuck with me in a lot of ways. I started wetting the bed, which led to harsh punishments from my mother. I spent a lot of time in a fantasy world. I think part of me hoped that if I left the DR, I could leave some of that pain behind me. So, in the end, I decided to go with my mom and Ricky to the United States.

The last days in the DR were a blur, and the next thing I knew, I was on a plane to Miami with my mom and my little brother. I cried the whole plane ride there. I was leaving behind most of the people I loved to go live in a strange place with people I didn't know at all. True, they were family, but they were strangers to me all the same.

When we got to Miami, we lived with some of my aunts and cousins. For seven months, we all slept in the living room of my aunt's house. Mom slept on the sofa with Ricky, and I slept on the living room floor. It was a sharp contrast to the comfort we had known in the DR, but I wanted to support my mom, so I kept quiet about it.

Gradually, I began to adjust. I was getting to know my aunts and cousins. I worked hard to acclimate to the new life I had before me and set out to try to make friends and improve my English. It was going pretty well. I became the man of the house, helping to look after my mother and brother and serving as a translator when needed.

Then, less than a year after arriving in Miami, my mom took us to New York City to visit her sister, who had fallen ill. She told us we would only be going for a little while, until her sister was well again. I didn't like New York City at all. It was dirty and gray and cold. It smelled like pee and garbage everywhere you went. It was nothing like I had experienced in the DR or in Miami. As soon as we arrived, I couldn't wait to leave. But we never did. My mom had decided to move us to New York, and there was really nothing I could do about it. Once again, my life was uprooted.

MY LIFE IN COLORS

7 years old living in DR

4

LIFE IN NEW YORK

I had a hard time getting used to the idea of making New York my home. We lived in Washington Heights, which is a community with a strong Dominican presence. Despite having family there and a shared sense of background in the community, it just never felt like home.

When it was time for me to start school, I was terrified. The taxi pulled up outside the public school, and I refused to get out. The school was a very rough place. I felt more out of place there than I had anywhere else before, and I was afraid they would kill me. Most of the time, I tried to roll with the punches and make the best out of things to help my mom out, but not this time. This time, I wouldn't budge. I would *not* be attending that school. My mom took me back home.

A friend suggested I might feel more comfortable at a school they knew about downtown called the Humanities School. I went to check it out and immediately felt more comfortable. The students were a mix of all backgrounds.

MY LIFE IN COLORS

There were not just other Latinos but also American, Chinese, Jewish, and all manner of other students. I was excited by the diversity. The school was focused more on acting, the arts, and the humanities and seemed much less aggressive than the public school uptown. The one catch was that it was on 18th Street, between 8th and 9th Avenue, which was a long way from where we lived in Washington Heights. This meant I would have to take several trains every day, both to and from school, but I didn't care. This was the school I knew I wanted to attend.

So that's what I did. I went to the Humanities School from 9th grade all the way through 12th grade. It was a good place for me. I took ESL classes with students from all over the world and was able to really improve my English. I made friends easily at that school. My closest friend was a Cuban girl named Delia. She was great. We were very different but became fast friends. My grades were good; hers weren't. She was a little rebellious, while I was absolutely not. I helped keep her in line, while she helped me venture out and experience new things. We were so close that many people assumed we were a couple.

Meanwhile, I knew I liked boys, but I didn't spend a lot of time thinking about it. At the time, I didn't even really know the term "gay." All I ever heard was the word "faggot." I was still my expressive self, but I fit in better at the Humanities School. People assumed Delia was a lesbian because she dressed in black, even though she wasn't. That didn't bother her, though. One teacher noticed us hanging around together and started asking us if we went to Church on the weekends. Me, having been raised Catholic (and being a little naïve) assumed that they meant *actual* church. It turns out they were talking about a queer dance club in the city. The teacher could sense my queerness (and assumed Delia's) and was trying in a subtle way to make us feel comfortable in ourselves. But I kept that part of myself so hidden that I didn't even really acknowledge it was there.

Although I was doing well at school, I still didn't like New York. I didn't have much of a social life outside of school. I would have to come straight home after school to help look after Ricky. My mother purchased a Latin dance club and was rarely home. She had a boyfriend I didn't particularly care for, and Ricky and I had to stay in our rooms whenever he was over. I never argued about it. I didn't want to rock the boat, and I always wanted to be there for my mom and my brother.

Meanwhile, Richard was having a rough time in the DR. He had fallen in with a bad crowd, quit going to school, and spent all his time partying. When my father moved in with a woman and started a new family, he left Richard behind in the old house. My mom went back to the DR to get him and bring him to live with us in New York.

Richard didn't do all that much better in New York than he did in the DR, except that he started going back to school. He didn't come to the Humanities School with me and instead decided to go to the public school, which was a pretty rough place. He and my mom fought constantly. He was not willing to adhere to the strict rules and curfews my mom wanted to set and was always in trouble for staying out too late and going to parties. Still, I liked having my brother back. Just like old times, he was always supportive and kind to me, and I realized how much I had missed him.

Despite the challenges at home, I worked really hard at school. I went on a school trip to Washington DC for three days to learn about the US government. My mom wasn't wild about the idea, but I somehow convinced her to let me go. The trip helped change some of my negative views about the United States. I started to understand some of the differences between the US and the DR, particularly with regard to women's rights. It inspired me to be a part of positive change in the world, and I became an activist. I started doing work to speak out against domestic violence and in support of women's rights.

As graduation approached, I was thinking more about my future. I wasn't sure yet what I wanted to do, but my hard work was paying off. I excelled in my classes and maintained a high GPA. I went in for a meeting with the guidance counselor, excited to start looking for a university. When I sat down at his desk, however, he presented me with a bunch of pamphlets for vocational and beauty schools. I left them on the desk and walked over to the stack of university pamphlets and started to leaf through them instead. The guidance counselor stopped me.

"Roberto," he said to me, "you wouldn't qualify for those schools."

"Why not?" I demanded. "I have a good GPA and have been a great student."

But the counselor pushed back. He told me I would be wasting my time at a four-year university. Basically, in no uncertain terms, he was convinced that pursuing university wasn't something suited for a person "like me."

I was upset, but I held it together in front of him. I thanked him for his time, told him I would figure it out for myself, and went straight to the school bathroom and cried. I had spent so much of my youth feeling like I wasn't enough, that I wasn't smart enough, fast enough, tall enough, skinny enough, handsome enough, *good* enough. But while I sat there, crying in the bathroom, I pushed back on those ideas for the first time in my life. I told myself I *was* better than that. It didn't matter if other people believed in me; I could believe in myself. I knew I could do more than the guidance counselor thought I could, and I set out to prove him wrong.

MY LIFE IN COLORS

MY LIFE IN COLORS

PART 3

CHRYSALIS

MY LIFE IN COLORS

MY LIFE IN COLORS

MY LIFE IN COLORS

With my best Friends (Diego and Marcos). Below photo, my oldest brother (Richard) and Ricky in NY while I was in Miami

5

COLLEGE YEARS

Since I didn't have much in the way of outside support, I decided to do my own research into what colleges I might attend. I needed a change, but I also wanted something that would be a little familiar, so I decided to look at schools in Miami. I applied to six different schools. A few sent me automatic acceptance letters, and a few others invited me to come out to Miami for an interview.

When I came to my mom and told her about my successes, I expected her to be happy for me. She wasn't. "You're not going to Miami," she told me. "You're staying here and going to Fordham University." She wanted me to stay and go to school in the Bronx so that I could continue to help take care of Ricky. She even offered to pay for my tuition. But I was determined. I knew that Miami was where I wanted to go. So I told my mother no.

She didn't take it well. She said if I moved out, that was it. I would be cut off completely. There would be no more support from her. At the time, it made me feel like she didn't love me. In hindsight, I understand it better. She felt like I was abandoning her and Ricky. She felt like she was losing me. I was her emotional support system and someone she could always count on. She would miss me. That was hard for her to accept. I wanted her to understand that this was something I needed to do for myself in order to grow, but she couldn't hear it.

I called my father to ask him what I should do. "What does your mother say?" he asked me. I told him she was dead set against it. There was still a bit of a rivalry between them, so, of course, he said yes. He flew out to meet me in Miami and took me to my university interviews. We visited five schools in one day, but the one that clicked for me was St. Thomas University. It was a small, private school, so it felt personal. It was also a Catholic school, so that felt familiar to me. It felt like home the moment I stepped on campus. But, as a private school, it was also very expensive. My dad offered to help, but I was also going to have to work hard to make it happen.

Back in New York, things were tenser with my mother. She wouldn't hear anything about my leaving and was adamant that I would receive no help from her. I went out to look for a job. I started out at McDonald's, but the pace was too crazy. I moved over to Wendy's and worked there for my entire senior year.

When the time came to leave for school, I had saved $2,000 for my move to Miami. I kept it in a shoebox in my closet. I thought I was rich and that I'd be able to buy my own car and rent my own apartment. Now, this was 1993. $2,000 went farther then but not *that* far. There was no way I was going to be able to afford a car, so I had to find another way to get down to Miami. Delia, who was moving to Miami with her family, told me about a bus I could take. The trick was that I needed my mother's signature to be able to get a ticket. Of course, that was out of the question, so I learned to forge her signature to get my ticket.

The day I was set to leave, I went to my mom's room to say goodbye. She wouldn't let me near her. "Just leave," was all she would say to me. It broke my heart. I started to cry and even thought about calling the whole thing off. But then Richard came to me. He was always my biggest supporter. When I graduated, he signed my yearbook saying "I am very happy that you graduated. Continue growing, continue to think positive and always be proud of who you are. OK little brother, from your oldest brother, Richard" That day, he took me by the shoulders and said, "You're going. Dry those tears. I believe in you. Don't be afraid; just go."

He sent me on my way with one suitcase in hand. As soon as I got on the bus, I started crying again. I was truly alone for the first time in my life, and I was terrified. There was an old woman sitting next to me, and, when she saw me crying, she asked me what was wrong. I told her my story, and she was very supportive and nurturing. She helped take care of me on the long bus ride to Miami. I was so young and naïve that I hadn't even packed any food for the trip. She shared her sandwich with me so that I would have something to eat. Twenty-four hours later, I was in Miami.

I arrived too early to move into the dorms, so I called my aunts to see if I could stay with them. My mom had already called them to say that I had abandoned her and Ricky. She had forbidden them from giving me a place to stay, but they felt sorry for me and let me come stay with them anyway. The whole time I was there, they tried to convince me to go back to my mother in New York, but I stood my ground.

Two days later, the campus opened, and I moved into my dorm room. Once I got there, I realized how ill-prepared I was. I didn't have any of the things I needed with me—no pillows, no towels, no bedsheets, nothing but the clothes I had packed. I used toilet paper after showers to dry myself off and slept on the bare bunk bed.

A week later, on family move-in day, I watched all the other kids arriving with their families. They were settling into their dorms with everything they needed. Seeing all those happy families making this big change together was too much. I locked myself in my room and cried. I felt stupid, naïve, and more alone than ever. But I was determined to get through it.

Eventually, my new roommate, Alonso, arrived with his family. Of course, I gathered myself together and was my usual polite and respectful self. I warmed up to his mother immediately. When she saw how little I had, she came back with a box containing a towel, a pillow, sheets, and everything else I needed. "You're my son too," she told me as she handed me the box. I thanked her and was so touched that, of course, I cried again.

Alonso and I bonded after that. We got along well and helped each other out in school. My major was still undecided, so my advisor helped me enroll in the basics. Looking at the course load, it seemed so generic and boring. I asked my advisor for one elective and selected Intro to Psychology. From the first class, I was hooked. I loved everything about psychology and knew that I wanted to make it my career. I joined the psychology club and started talking to the professors to try to learn everything I could about what they do. I made sure to smile, ask questions, and show interest at every opportunity.

I was thriving academically, but I still felt emotionally isolated. I had little to no communication with my mom. My dad, while invested in what I was doing, was occupied with his new family. I tried to smile through it and set out to make friends with my peers. I was very agreeable and outgoing, which made me very likable. I wanted so badly to be accepted. The best way I knew how to do that was not to rock the boat. It worked, and before long I made a group of friends.

I continued to focus on my studies. I had A's and B's in all of my classes, except for a D in Statistics, which I ended up retaking at a community college and transferring over to keep my GPA up. I worked hard and was able to graduate in three years instead of four. After completing my bachelor's degree, I decided I wanted to pursue my doctorate in psychology, even though I was afraid that I wasn't good enough. I pushed aside my fears and applied to Carlos Albizu University, a Hispanic college that offered the degree I wanted, and I got in. I was there for a semester and got good grades, but I didn't feel like I had learned a thing. It wasn't as challenging as I was used to at St. Thomas, so I transferred back. St. Thomas didn't offer a doctorate in psychology, so I decided to pursue a master's degree in marriage and family therapy instead.

It turned out to be the best decision I could have made. When I returned to St. Thomas for my master's degree, I ended up meeting a few mentors who would play a pivotal role in my professional development. The first was Dr. Susan Angulo. She admired me for my direct (and loud) communication and took me under her wing. I started working as her assistant, and I learned so much from her.

In one class, another mentor, Dr. Barbara Buzzi, gave us an assignment to study a family member to learn about family secrets and family dynamics. It was recommended that we interview the oldest member of our family, so I reached out to my Mama Nana. At first, I was worried it would be uncomfortable, but we sat together for hours and talked. It was easy and natural. I got a lot of information and family secrets from her, and we bonded. Turns out, I was one of her favorite grandchildren. She could see how sensitive and emotional I was but could also see that I had the strength to say whatever was on my mind. She knew that would cause me pain but also that it would help me do great things. She loved me because she knew that I would struggle and that I would come out on the other side of it stronger. She became one of my biggest supporters. I always felt completely safe and loved when I was with her.

Around the same time, I also got my first job working in the field as a domestic violence counselor. Technically, I needed a master's degree for the position, but I had worked out a deal where I could start working while pursuing my degree. I was to receive reduced pay until my degree was complete. While there, I met Dr. E-Thel Taylor, a licensed mental health counselor and marriage and family therapist. She was a little bit eccentric, and people tended to steer clear of her, so, naturally, I gravitated toward her. I asked her if I could shadow her and learn from her, and she agreed.

I was in awe of the way she carried herself. She was a tiny woman, but she took no shit from anyone. She was Jewish and had survived a concentration camp, which left her fearless. She worked in the domestic violence unit, where she would have to confront the batterers. She was never afraid of them, despite the fact that they were often huge men twice her size. She was always kind to her patients, even if they had done some terrible things. Because of this, she was able to get information from them without being perceived as a threat. It was an amazing thing to watch her work.

Dr. Taylor was instrumental in pushing me in my career. She encouraged me to pursue licenses in both marriage and family therapy and mental health, which she knew would open up many more doors for me. She had faith that I could do it. She pushed me to leave the domestic violence center and get experience working in different places. I started working in hospitals with children to learn about developmental therapy. I also began working with the LGBT community and got certified in HIV/AIDS support. I worked in family court as a mental health expert talking with judges. It was intimidating at first, but it taught me a lot. Dr. Taylor's guidance was instrumental in my becoming who I am, and I'm so glad I listened to her.

College Years - in our Apartment

1st - trip to Key West just moved to FL from NY

Mom and I right after my undergraduate graduation 1996

6

COMING OUT

Of course, going to a Catholic university in Miami, in many ways, I stayed close to my roots. My roots in the Dominican Republic and in Catholicism both adhere to very traditional values. Gender roles and expectations for how a person should live their life are laid out very clearly: Women are expected to get married and be caretakers, and men are expected to be macho. Men shouldn't be too emotional, too creative, or too expressive; instead, they should play sports (preferably baseball) and provide for their families.

I didn't fit into these traditional gender roles at all. I *was* creative and emotional and expressive. I had no interest whatsoever in following the paths that were laid out for me. Because I was going against these traditions, I had no real role models for how to build my life. There was no one around me in my daily life that looked or acted like me, so I assumed there was no one around me who felt like me. It made me feel very alone.

MY LIFE IN COLORS

I remember I took a gender roles class in high school, and one day we were asked to switch gender roles to learn through first-hand experience. For the assignment, I wore a dress to school. My mother did *not* like that. She didn't understand why I would do such a thing. Like me, she wasn't raised with any frame of reference for what going against traditional gender roles would look like. Even though dressing like a woman was not something I felt like I wanted to do in my daily life, I was very interested in being in touch with the feminine sides of myself. After my mother's reaction, I learned to hide that side of myself from her. In general, I kept many things about myself suppressed. I always knew I liked boys, but because of how I was raised, I just assumed that feeling in me was the devil. Whenever I had those feelings, I tried to distract myself. I would start praying or doing anything else I could to bury those feelings away.

When I went to college in Miami, I continued to keep that part of myself under wraps. I was so focused on my schooling that I didn't even think about romantic relationships or going out. I just wanted to work hard and do well. Plus, I was going to a Catholic school, so it wasn't like being gay was widely accepted there either. Still, being my outgoing self, it was easy for me to make friends. Just like in high school, I became friends with a girl in college who pursued me and wanted to be my girlfriend. Even though I wasn't really interested in her that way, I didn't want to hurt her feelings, so I said yes.

But I wasn't fooling everyone. I had a friend who was gay and could recognize that in me from a mile away. One night, he invited me to go out to a club called O-Zone with him. I didn't know what kind of club it was. When we got inside, I looked around and noticed it was mostly guys. I realized where we were and started to get really nervous but also excited. I stayed frozen by the entrance and just started counting people. There were more than 200 people in this club—all people *like me*. It was the first time I had seen such a gathering of openly gay men, and it was completely overwhelming. For the first time in my life, I didn't feel like I was alone. It felt amazing.

As I was standing by the entrance, I saw this man come in. It was Ariel. It was my first time seeing him, and I was totally taken aback. There was something about him that just drew me to him like a tractor beam. I couldn't control it. It was love at first sight. As ever, I am not shy, so I said hello to him immediately. Because I was standing by the door, he thought I was the bouncer. A cute bouncer, in fact. He started checking me out, but I was oblivious, so I totally missed the cue. I didn't know what to say next, but I wanted to talk to him more, so I just said, "Nice pants." Ariel smiled but walked away, and we didn't talk the rest of the night. I just stayed where I was by the door, taking it all in.

On the way home from the club, my friend took me home and was worried I didn't have a good time. "You didn't even dance or drink!" he said. But I did have a good time. A great time, in fact. It had opened up something inside of me, so I turned to him and said, "I think I like boys." It was the first time I had ever said it out loud to anyone. It was an awesome feeling. It was a freeing feeling. My friend confided in me that he knew the whole time, but because I had a girlfriend, he said he would keep my secret.

Well, he didn't. He outed me to our friends. But by this time, I was ready to be honest with them. I didn't deny it. Seeing all those people in the club—out, happy, living their lives without shame—gave me the courage that I needed to come out. The first thing I did was talk to my girlfriend. At first, she pushed back and tried to convince me that I actually liked girls too, but I was committed to living my life authentically. We broke up amicably and remained friends.

My gay friend kept inviting me out with him after that. I met a tall, handsome pilot at a restaurant who invited me on a date. I agreed, but on the date, I just wasn't connecting with him. While we were together, I looked across the bar and who did I see but Ariel? He was standing on the other side of the bar with a friend. Immediately, that same tractor beam attraction kicked in, and I wanted to go over to him. So, with my usual lack of filter, I turned to the pilot and said, "Thank you for the drink and the ride, but this isn't going to work out. I'm afraid you're going to want to kiss me, and

I just don't want to do that." He got up and left me without a ride home, but I didn't care. I went over to talk to Ariel.

I said hello to Ariel and his friend and asked his friend to dance. I really wanted to dance with Ariel but felt nervous. As I went out to the dance floor, I turned around to see that Ariel had followed me out. "I know you didn't ask me," he said, "and I don't really dance, but I wanted to dance with you." I told him he was the one I really wanted to dance with anyway, and we danced. I was falling in love.

We took things organically and slow. We went on a date but didn't kiss. We were just getting to know each other. After the date, Ariel took me home to where I was staying with one of my cousins. I had butterflies in my stomach after spending time with Ariel, and I decided to come out to my cousin to tell him I was gay. Like so many people before, he tried to convince me that I wasn't really gay, that I was just mistaken, but I wouldn't deny it anymore. Things escalated from insults into a physical altercation resulting in me leaving the house.

After that, I had nowhere to go, and I lived in my car for three days. I was battered, and I felt completely ashamed. I didn't go to school because I didn't want anyone to see me that way. Professors were calling me, asking where I was. It wasn't like me to miss school. Eventually, I called Delia because I needed to see someone. When I told her what had happened with my cousin, she said she always knew I was gay and invited me to come stay with her for a few days. Then, I moved in with my aunt, Orly, who was very supportive. Her kindness and love gave me the courage to come out to the rest of my family.

After that, I invited my mother and my father to Miami, separately, because they didn't want to see each other. I told my father first, and he took it very well. He was very kind but obviously worried about me. He looked at me and said, "Robelín, I know you're going to make it because you work very hard and you're very smart. But be careful. The world can be a beautiful place, but there are people in it who might want to do you harm. You can be naïve, so be careful of people." I knew what he meant, and I felt very loved.

My mother came after my father left. She took the news badly. At first, she refused to accept it. She brought up the girlfriends I had had and tried to convince me I wasn't gay. She wanted to know who to blame. She left angry, and it took her a long time to come around. Despite her reaction, I knew that she loved me and that she meant well. She was just repeating the patterns she was raised with and wanted to protect me. She didn't know how to do it any other way.

As I came out to the rest of my family, they each had their own reaction. Some were very accepting, whether they fully understood it or not. Some were less accepting. They expressed worries that I would start living life dressed as a woman or that I would die of AIDS. But I was committed to living my life fully as myself, and so that's what I set out to do. And even though it was hard, it felt good.

MY LIFE IN COLORS

My second mom, Caridad and I. Ariel's mom. LOVE HER SO MUCH. She is in heaven!

MY LIFE IN COLORS

7

FINDING MYSELF

I adjusted well to my life as an openly gay man. For me, it was natural. I felt more comfortable living honestly and being unashamed of who I was. My relationship with Ariel was getting stronger as well, but Ariel was not out. We developed a secret language using beeper codes to communicate with each other on the sly. Eventually, it got to the point where Ariel was staying over every night, so I invited him to move in with me. Ariel agreed but did so without telling anyone we were in a relationship.

At the time, I was living in an efficiency apartment, so we didn't have a lot of space. We didn't have a lot of money either. Still, we had a wonderful time together. Ariel decorated the place and made a nice home for us. Everything felt totally natural. We had an easy intimacy between us, even though we were opposite in many ways. We had so much fun together. We never did crazy things—no drugs, no alcohol, no smoking, but we didn't need them.

We had each other, and that was enough. I knew I didn't want to date anyone else.

On our first vacation together, we went to Key West. We had reserved a beautiful hotel by the water and were excited to spend time together. When we arrived at the hotel, we were shocked to find everyone by the pool was completely naked. We had accidentally reserved a room at a nudist LGBT hotel. Now, neither Ariel nor I are a very into PDA, nor are we the type to run around naked in public. We were the only people in the hotel with their clothes on. Despite that, we had a wonderful time and explored all over the area. Even though we weren't married, it felt like a honeymoon. We connected on a deep level, and we knew we could be happy seeing each other every day of our lives.

Eventually, we realized we needed more space than our efficiency apartment had to offer us, but we couldn't afford it on our own. We ended up moving into a two-bedroom apartment with an old childhood friend of mine, Marcos. Marcos was a lovely person and a lot of fun. He was funny and outgoing, but he lived a very different lifestyle from Ariel and me. Marcos was wild and often partied late into the night. People were constantly coming and going from the apartment. Meanwhile, Ariel and I were forming our own tribe of friends who became our family. So, as much as Marcos, Ariel and I all liked each other, the arrangement only lasted a year before Ariel and I moved out.

MY LIFE IN COLORS

A friend of ours was selling her one-bedroom apartment. Even though we didn't have a lot of money at the time, she accepted our modest offer on her apartment. We ended up living there together for seven years. Ariel went back to school online to get his bachelor's degree, which was a huge accomplishment. He was the first person in his family to get a degree, just like I was, and I was so proud of him. As we both started doing better professionally, we made more money and lived a very comfortable life together.

Since I was out, I introduced Ariel to my family. Not everyone in my family was accepting, but I told them that, while they could say whatever they wanted to me, they were *never* to express any negative feelings to Ariel. Everyone respected that. They were very kind and welcoming to Ariel, which meant a lot to me. My Mama Nana, who loved me dearly but never really understood the gay thing, accepted Ariel with open arms. "Whoever you love," she told me, "I'm going to love too."

MY LIFE IN COLORS

MY LIFE IN COLORS

1st - in mexico
2nd - with friends Alina and Ana

MY LIFE IN COLORS

*Disney World in FL
with a friend, Diego, who passed away due to cancer.*

8

CHALLENGES ALONG THE WAY

Even though, in many ways, my life was going well, things are never always sunshine and roses.

In 1995, not long after I had come out, my father died unexpectedly. He was out for a run when he had a heart attack. It was my first time experiencing a major loss, and it was completely overwhelming. I couldn't function. I loved my father so much, and it was hard to accept that such a kind, loving, and gentle person in my life was suddenly absent from it. Even though, at the time, Ariel and I had only been seeing each other for a few months, he took care of me through my grief. He helped me get ready to go to the DR for the funeral and was waiting for me when I got back.

I had a lot of trouble adjusting to the grief. I was working two jobs and going to school, nearing graduation. It was something I had been working so hard toward, and now my father wouldn't see it happen. I got very depressed. I couldn't focus, couldn't eat, couldn't do anything. Ariel stayed strong by my side, and I started to see a psychiatrist.

I was prescribed medication to help me through, but I decided not to take it right away. Instead, I worked through the grief with the support of my psychiatrist and my loved ones. Eventually, I started to learn how to live with the grief and move forward in life.

But it wasn't long before my brother, Richard, started having some serious problems. He had become an actor and was working in telenovelas. He traveled a lot for work but would come to Miami often to visit. He and I talked on the phone all the time. He was always very loving and worked hard to make sure all of us siblings stayed in touch. He had a rebellious soul, but he had a good heart.

I was the first to notice his drug addiction. It was easy for him to hide in his industry, but my training as a therapist alerted me to the warning signs. I came to Richard's wife and our mom with my concerns. We arranged to have an intervention for Richard with a therapist, but Richard wouldn't go. The three of us met with the therapist anyway, and they recommended that we take Richard to detox, so that's what we did.

Over the years, Richard was in and out of five different treatment programs. He would attend, do well, and it would work for a while, but he would always relapse. Each time he relapsed, I would call him. Usually, I would have to leave a message.

"Hey, I hope you're OK," I would tell him on the answering machine, "but you need to come home. We love you. It doesn't matter how many times you fall; we will help you back up. Just come home, please."

He would call me back, high as a kite. Hearing him that way would always make me cry. I was so worried about him. Richard, as ever, would try to protect me. He would tell me not to cry and promise to come home. He wouldn't let me come to get him because he was worried it would be too dangerous for me, but he would find someone to give him a ride.

It went on like that for a while, but addictions can be terrible monsters. I learned as much as I could about substance abuse to try to help him, but his addictions just grew worse. He was skinny as a rail, and his arms were covered in track marks. Our mother and I got together to try to find a way to help him. We learned about a wilderness program back in the DR. He would be gone for six months, and he would have absolutely no contact with anyone outside the program. He tried to escape several times, but the place was so remote that he had nowhere to run, so he always went back.

When he came back from the program, he looked good. He looked stronger and more centered. We were hopeful that it had worked. He had to stay separated from his wife since he didn't know how to be in a relationship with her when he wasn't using, so I took out a $50,000 loan to have our mom's garage converted into an apartment space for him. For a while, he was happy and doing well.

But then, he started doing telenovelas again. He would disappear for days at a time. One day, he called me, upset, admitting he had relapsed. As usual, I comforted him, and he told me that he was coming home. He never did.

It was Mother's Day, and we had planned a huge party for our mom at her house. I was in my home office when I got a call from the police. They said they needed me to come identify the body of my brother. They had found him, and all he had in his wallet was his ID and my business card. I didn't accept that it could be him. It was Mother's Day, and he had promised to be there for our mom. He was *always* there for the family. It *couldn't* be him.

But it was. He had killed himself with an overdose. I was completely distraught. I couldn't handle seeing my brother, my best friend from the day I was born, lying there, cold. He looked so fragile and alone. I had to collect myself. I knew I had to go to our mother and tell her what had happened.

I walked in the door, faced with my impossible task. She was all dressed up for the party, and she looked so beautiful. I couldn't even look at her. She knew what had happened without me saying anything.

"What happened?" she said but then quickly covered with, "No. No, I don't want to know."

She knew but couldn't accept it. She wouldn't even let me hug her. She just kept saying, "Where's Richard? Where is he?" It broke my heart to see her like that. It still makes me cry to think about it.

But as broken as my heart was, I had to function. Someone had to make the funeral arrangements and get things together. So that's what I did. Again, Ariel stayed by my side through the grief. I knew my brother had wanted to be buried close to his daughters, but my mom insisted that he be buried in the DR near our father.

Standing in front of his coffin at the final viewing in Miami, I talked to my brother. "I don't understand any of it," I told him, "And I'm sorry I failed you. But I am *angry* with you right now. I know you were suffering, but you left me. I am going to miss you. I *do* miss you. I hope you are in a better place, with Dad." And then I walked away to return to Miami.

The time after my brother's death was very difficult. Sometimes, the grief was so painful I could hardly breathe. I needed something to occupy my time, so I decided to go back to school in my brother's honor. I made up my mind to finally go and pursue my doctorate. It was a difficult process that cost me blood, sweat, and tears, but the effort helped me move through my grief.

These early experiences with the difficult sides of life helped strengthen Ariel and my relationship. But, as good as we were together, things were not perfect. Ariel was still not out, and, over the years, that began to take its toll. It was a difficult experience to feel so close to someone but to have to stay distant around others. It was hard to share a life with him part of the time while having to stay out of the way the rest of the time. I had to hide when Ariel's family was around. That hurt. Ariel had been so accepted into my family, but I didn't have the same luxury from his.

Part of me could understand Ariel's fears of coming out. He came from a very traditional Cuban family. To date me, a black man (even another Latino), we would have to fight through generations of racism and homophobia. But I knew I could win them over if I just had the chance. I had faced some of the same homophobia in my family, but I fought for Ariel . . . for *us*. I worked hard to make sure he was accepted into my family, and because of that, he was. I took all of their ignorant and hateful comments and shielded Ariel from them. I made sure they knew that what he and I were doing wasn't wrong; it was simply love. I wanted him to do the same for me.

After five years, the hiding had become too much. I was tired of feeling invisible. I gave Ariel an ultimatum: Either you come out and tell your family about us, or we're done.

"I love you," I told him, "but either you tell them, or I have to go."

But Ariel still wasn't ready, so I left. We still loved each other completely, but I couldn't live that life anymore. We broke up, but we still had the property together to sort out. I told Ariel that this was the deal: I had made the down payment on the apartment, so I would keep it. I gave him a date to move out. In exchange, he could take whatever he wanted with him when he left.

MY LIFE IN COLORS

On the day he moved out, Ariel called his brothers to help him get his stuff. When I came home to the apartment later that day, everything was gone. He left me nothing but one sofa. Ariel's brothers had convinced him to take everything else. I was devastated. It felt like I was starting my life over from scratch. I sat on the couch in the empty apartment and cried for hours.

It was difficult being apart from Ariel. I was completely heartbroken, but I knew I deserved better than a life of hiding myself from people who should be my family. My friend, Carmen, invited me to go with her on a trip to Italy to try to lift my spirits. I had never been to Europe before, and even though I didn't feel like doing much of anything, I knew it wasn't good for me to wallow in my heartbreak, so I went.

We were in Italy for 15 days. It was a beautiful and romantic place, and the food was amazing, but it mostly made me miss Ariel. I met a man there, and we had a little fling, but he wasn't Ariel. It wasn't love.

When I came back from Italy, I started working on my doctorate. The heartbreak was taking its toll. I couldn't eat, and I started losing a lot of weight. I was down to 115 pounds and finally went to a doctor. I had become anemic. I needed to start eating more, but it was hard with everything I had going on.

Meanwhile, my mom had stayed in touch with Ariel. By this time, she had already accepted him as a son, and she knew how much we loved each other. She told Ariel that he and I belonged together but that I wouldn't take him back unless he made a place for me in his life. One day, my mom invited me over to her house, and, to my surprise, Ariel was there. By this time, we had been apart for six months. Ariel came up to me and asked, "Do you love me?" I told him, tearfully, that I did. He agreed to come out.

When Ariel came out to his family, he did it alone. It was a very dramatic scene. His family threatened to find me and kill me. But he held strong and kept working to make them accept us and our relationship. He invited us all to a restaurant so that they could meet me over dinner. I made sure to sit next to his mother so that I could work my magic on her, and it worked like a charm. From that moment on, she saw that we were good people, and we became super close.

The next step was to win over Ariel's father. It would be more of a challenge. I knew he was very macho, but despite that, I hugged him before he could say no. I worked hard to gain his acceptance. I learned how to make Cuban coffee and would make it whenever he came to visit. Eventually, I succeeded in winning him over. Only a few months after Ariel's coming out, Ariel's father came to me and said, "You are good for my son. You have our blessings." We finally felt like a complete family, and it was an amazing feeling.

MY LIFE IN COLORS

MY LIFE IN COLORS

MY LIFE IN COLORS

PART 3

BUTTERFLY

MY LIFE IN COLORS

Paris France 2019

MY LIFE IN COLORS

Paris - France 2019

MY LIFE IN COLORS

In my 40's at home - BDAY DAY

MY LIFE IN COLORS

Loving myself above all - accepting all the colors of the rainbow

MY LIFE IN COLORS

MY LIFE IN COLORS

MY LIFE IN COLORS

9

MY LIFE

After we began to live our lives completely in the open, everything got even better. It felt like a storybook. Knowing we had the support of our families was huge for us, and we felt invincible. We were free to be ourselves fully, and our life was filled with love and respect and nurturing. Because of that, sex and intimacy in our relationship went through the roof. We knew we were destined to spend the rest of our lives together.

Now, Ariel and I have been together for 28 years. Eventually, we sold the apartment and bought a house together. We have four dogs, Zuki, Oki, Zia, and Yoshi, and a cat named Missy. We adore each and every one of them. Ariel and I support each other fully and are proud of one another's accomplishments. We have traveled the world together and have seen so many wonderful things. Even though we are total opposites, we complement each other perfectly. I love to cook; he doesn't. He loves to garden, whereas I prefer to stay away from the dirt. But because of our differences, we have built a beautiful home together.

When gay marriage legalization passed, we were both so happy. I, of course, wanted to get married right away. I'm always the type to go all-out, while Ariel likes to fly more under the radar.

"Why would we need to get married?" Ariel said. "We've already got everything we need."

"What do you mean?" I said. "Of course we need to get married!"

So on May 18th, 2018, we went to the courthouse, got the application, and got married. We both cried that day. Being seen as a human being, not having to hide any part of ourselves, and being able to live our lives fully in the open . . . it meant so much. Some of our family members were happy, and some weren't, but that didn't matter to us. We could agree to disagree on this issue and move on with our lives.

Even though our families still don't always understand each other, we are happy. I have six wonderful godchildren, whom I love with all my heart: Nolan, Maia, Edwin, Ervin, Chantal, and Cesar. I remember when Edwin was born; I loved him from the moment I met him. I had always joked that Ariel and I were going to adopt a Chinese baby one day. When I held Edwin in my arms for the first time, I just looked at him and said, "This is not exactly what I ordered, but this will do." He's been like a son to me from that moment on.

MY LIFE IN COLORS

Of course, life is not always perfect. Some years back, Ariel's father, Alipio, was diagnosed with colon cancer. He only survived three months after the diagnosis. By this time, Ariel's father trusted me enough to help with all his medical care, and we bonded even more. He even told me I was his son and gave me kisses. It meant so much to be accepted by him so completely. Growing from "I don't want to see you because you're black and you're gay," to being told "you're my son" was a huge moment for me.

Ariel's mother, Caridad, was diagnosed with cancer not long after Alipio passed. She was on chemo for a long time, and it was a hard road, and she ultimately lost her battle. They had both become my parents too, so it was a terrible loss to suffer. But through it all, Ariel and I have learned that, together, we can face anything.

In 2020, I began to face some medical issues of my own. Just as the pandemic was starting, I started to feel severely fatigued. I was getting acne and losing my voice frequently. I knew something was wrong, so I went to several doctors to try to figure it out. I had trouble finding attentive care. One doctor even assumed it was likely AIDS, even though I had been in a committed relationship with one man for over 20 years. He was dismissive of my health just because I was gay. My condition kept worsening, and flare-ups even prevented me from being able to work.

Eventually, I found a doctor who took the time to really find out what was wrong with me. He spent four hours with me, running tests and asking questions. He diagnosed me with an IGG deficiency auto-immune disorder. I did research into the disorder and found a community online. When the doctor recommended that I start a series of infusions, the members of the community advised against it due to the risk of complications. My doctor respected my wishes, and I decided to implement some lifestyle changes instead. I have cut out dairy, gluten, and sugar from my diet. I started a course of natural therapy treatments, sauna treatments, and other nutritional and health-based practices. They have worked wonders for my condition and have even helped clear up the IBS I had struggled with for years. Even though it hasn't been easy, this journey has taught me that you have to push boundaries, ask questions, and find what works for you.

MY LIFE IN COLORS

Me with Edwin at Disney World in FL

Netherlands with my godson Edwin

MY LIFE IN COLORS

Paris

Trip with Edwin - Amsterdam

Bestfriends: Angie and Willie
Me in Key west FL
Me in Redwood Park in CA

MY LIFE IN COLORS

MY LIFE IN COLORS

MY LIFE IN COLORS

Trip with Edwin - Amsterdam

MY LIFE IN COLORS

MY LIFE IN COLORS

10

MY WORK

Most often, the path that works for me has not been a straight line. The work that I do professionally has been no different. I've always been a creative and expressive person, but I was raised with the notion that nothing creative could become a career. I was always told to stop dreaming and to get my head out of the clouds. Though I never fully embraced this idea, it did stick with me. The best outlet I found for my expressiveness was the mental health sector.

I had always been a natural advocate. Whenever I would hear of discrimination, I would want to fight against it. Unfortunately, discrimination exists everywhere, even amongst mental health counselors. When I first encountered discrimination in my field, I was working at a non-profit agency where I heard some counselors discussing how disgusted they were by their lesbian patients. I marched straight into the office of my supervisor and I demanded to be trained on how to work with and better support

LGBTQ patients. I used what I learned to train other counselors as well.

Over the years, I've worked hard to provide a broad spectrum of care for all of the clients I've come into contact with. I have done work not only in counseling but also in community care, case management, and many other related fields. I have worked with a wide variety of clients from all backgrounds and walks of life. It's important to me to try to understand my clients and meet them wherever they're at.

My work eventually brought me to a Health Advisory company, where I worked as a medical advisor for 13 years. The work that I did there was very different from the work I had done in the past, but it was interesting. Technically, I was not fully qualified for the position since I wasn't a medical doctor or a nurse, but, true to my nature, I applied anyway. They flew me out to Baltimore for an interview. While I was there, I was brought into a meeting room with 15 people in it. I turned on the charm, and everything was going well. We were clicking until they learned I was Dominican and started to talk to me about baseball. Now, as you might guess, I'm not a big sports fan, so I went to the bathroom to Google some baseball facts so I could hold up my end of the conversation. I ended up getting the job.

I was to focus on the mental health side of medical advising. In this job, I would be paired up with clients, usually wealthy families, who would meet with me for a health assessment. That assessment would be passed on to other professionals in their lives to help them continue with their care. The work was challenging but not as emotionally taxing as therapy work, and, for the most part, I enjoyed it.

While working there, I met Angie Mendez, who was assigned to train me as a health advisor. We didn't click at first. I was such an open book, whereas Angie was a bit more guarded. In time, we came to trust each other and grew very close. I observed how she carried herself with grace and faced any challenge that came her way with self-respect and dignity. I really respected that. She taught me that there are many ways to be resilient. In time, we became best friends. We even worked to open a business together, Global Animal Services, which helps connect people with service animals. Ariel and I have also become close with her husband, Willie, who once told me, "Just be fearless and you can do anything. Trust yourself." And like magic, the gates of opportunity opened up for me.

However, due to my health struggles in recent years, I ended up losing the job that I had as a private health advisor for. They weren't able to provide me with the support and flexibility that I needed to work through my health issues. So, I decided to set out to dedicated 100% of my time to my private practice for the first time in my career.

Carving my own path through my career was scary at times, but it paid off in the end. Now I have a 100% private practice. I can support myself and my family completely independently and am able to provide services to my clients on my own terms. I am very proud of all I have learned and how that has given me the ability to have close contact with my clients to provide them with a personal level of care. I cultivate an environment of mutual understanding and complete honesty with my clients, and for those where that clicks, I am able to provide an extremely high standard of care.

Throughout my journey I have met many people who believed in me and help me become who I am today. I have learned a lot about myself through the way they see me. Various mentors have written recommendations for me, and I have learned to appreciate more aspects of myself through their words. In their letters, they have highlighted that I am a giving individual, who can serve as a resource, a guide and a hard worker. I have the ability to work with diverse populations, including non-voluntary clients in difficult circumstances. They have marked my undeniable passion for helping others and my strong interpersonal skills. They recognize that I am a loyal and dedicated individual who is committed, self-driven and high performing. I have been recognized as a strong leader who is able to motivate my team through my positive attitude, unlimited creativity and boundless energy. On a more personal note, they have noted that am trustworthy, values-driven and relentlessly motivated to actualize myself as both a person and as a professional.

One of the most rewarding aspects of my job is the fact that I can help people realize that they always have options. A person can change their reality by learning to change the way they think. You and you alone have control of your reality. You can't control what life sends your way, but you can control how you respond to it. You can depend on yourself, and you don't need to rely on external sources to find happiness. The ability to help people feel comfortable enough about themselves to put themselves first, just like I had to learn to do for myself, is something I love about my work.

ME AT HOME - WORKING

MY LIFE IN COLORS

MY LIFE IN COLORS

11

WORDS OF WISDOM

The rainbow flag is an important symbol for me, and it carries many meanings. It has significance for its shared meanings of identity, sexuality, race, emotion, and different lives lived. But it also has some personal significance.

When my father passed, I felt so many things all at once. I was angry, I was depressed, and I was grieving. Some family members had told me that my coming out as gay led to his heart attack. While I didn't truly believe that, I couldn't help but feel guilt as well.

One day, when I felt like I was drowning in my pain and anger, I spoke out to my father's spirit. I said to him, "Dad, I'm angry. You were only 42. I don't know how we left things between us. Was it my fault? Please, can you just give me a sign that you love me?"

Then, on my way back from work, a rainbow appeared in the sky. Somehow, I knew that was a message from my dad. It was his way of saying, "Hey kid, I love you. It's not your fault that I'm gone. It was just my time. I'm still your dad, and I'm still here in my own way." From that moment on, any time I feel like I need my father's support, I see a rainbow. Every time.

This is how I believe in God. God is in nature. God is in kindness. God is in the warmth of the sun and in nourishment. I believe in a God with no gender and no preconceived notions of what love should look like, as long as it is real love. My Catholic family pushes back on these ideas, but this is what makes sense to me. And this has served me well.

My life now is good, but the road to get here has not always been easy. I have experienced heavy loss, sexual abuse, homophobia, racism, loneliness, and so many other difficult things along the way. But, even though I have struggled in my life, these struggles have helped shape who I have become. I don't see myself as a victim but as a survivor. Life is often hard, but you can choose what you say to yourself and how you face the challenges you are dealt.

The most important thing you can do is get to know yourself. Listen to yourself and follow your heart. Learn to trust yourself and how to become your own biggest advocate. Have confidence in yourself and your ability to overcome any situation. Even if right now you feel like you are alone or you feel like you are not enough, remember that you *are* enough. You always have been enough, and you

always will be enough. Believe in yourself, work hard, be resilient, stay humble, and great things can happen to you.

Whenever you start to hear negative words creep their way into your thoughts, replace them with positive ones. Find a mantra of your own. **Remind yourself of the following things: I am lovable. I am significant. I matter. I have something to offer the world. I am smart. I am healthy. I can choose. I am enough.**

The words that we tell ourselves are the most important. If we consistently deliver these messages to ourselves and start to believe them, we can change our realities. Make better choices, and your life *will* change. Believe in yourself, and you can do *anything*. And I am living proof.

I am at a place now where I love my life. I love my friends and family. I love myself. I look at each morning as a new beginning and embrace the positives from every experience.

Thank you for taking the time to read these small parts of my still-unfolding narrative. I wish you all a **rainbow**!

MY LIFE IN COLORS

Ariel and Me at home

Story Terrace

www.ingramcontent.com/pod-product-compliance
Lightning Source LLC
LaVergne TN
LVHW061529070526
838199LV00009B/431